LIVEWIRE REAL LIVES

Isaac Ne[illegible]

Brandon Robshaw and Rochelle Scholar

Published in association with The Basic Skills Agency

Hodder & Stoughton

A MEMBER OF THE HODDER HEADLINE GROUP

Acknowledgements

Cover: Darren Lock

Illustrations: Mike Bell

Photo, p.27: © Dean and Chapter, Westminster

Every effort has been made to trace copyright holders of material reproduced in this book. Any rights not acknowledged will be acknowledged in subsequent printings if notice is given to the publisher.

Orders; please contact Bookpoint Ltd, 39 Milton Park, Abingdon, Oxon OX14 4TD. Telephone: (44) 01235 400414, Fax: (44) 01235 400454. Lines are open from 9.00–6.00, Monday to Saturday, with a 24 hour message answering service.
Email address: orders@bookpoint.co.uk

British Library Cataloguing in Publication Data
A catalogue record for this title is available from the British Library

ISBN 0 340 77416 9

First published 2000
Impression number 10 9 8 7 6 5 4 3 2 1
Year 2005 2004 2003 2002 2001 2000

Typeset by GreenGate Publishing Services, Tonbridge, Kent.
Printed in Great Britain for Hodder and Stoughton Educational, a division of Hodder Headline Plc, 338 Euston Road, London NW1 3BH, by Redwood Books, Trowbridge, Wilts

Contents

1 The Apple

A young man was sitting in an orchard.
Suddenly, an apple fell from a tree.
Most people would take no notice.
Or perhaps they would pick the apple up
and eat it.

But this young man started thinking.
Why did the apple fall?
Of course, everyone knows that
things fall down
if nothing holds them up.
But why?

An idea came to the young man.
The apple fell because the Earth pulled it.
The Earth pulled the apple towards it
like a magnet pulls iron towards it.
The young man thought of a name
for this force.
He called it gravity.

The young man thought some more.
If an apple is pulled down to the Earth,
why isn't the moon?
Nothing is holding the moon up.
Why doesn't it fall?

Another idea came to the young man.
Earth's gravity does pull the moon.
But it doesn't fall,
because it is already moving.
Without the Earth's gravity,
the moon would fly off into space.
Instead, it goes around the Earth,
held in place by Earth's gravity.

In the same way,
the young man realised,
the Earth goes around the sun.
The sun's gravity holds it in place.

Everything has gravity –
a force that pulls other objects towards it.
The bigger the object,
the stronger its gravity.

The young man's name was Isaac Newton.
He was 23 years old.
He had just made
one of the greatest discoveries
in the history of science.

2 Early Days

Isaac Newton was born
on Christmas Day, in 1642.
He was born in the village of Woolsthorpe,
in Lincolnshire.
His father had been a small farmer.
But Isaac never knew his father.
His father died three months before
Isaac was born.

Isaac nearly died, too.
He was a small, weak baby.
The midwife did not expect him to live.
He was so small, the story goes,
that he could fit into a two-pint pot
(about a litre).
But he survived
and grew into a healthy little boy.

When Isaac was three,
his mother married again.
Her new husband did not want Isaac
to live with them.
So Isaac was left with his grandmother.

Being left by his mother
must have hurt Isaac very much.
For the rest of his life,
he was always shy and lonely.
He found it hard to trust people.
He never made friends easily.
He never got married.

Isaac went to the local school.
He didn't make any close friends there,
but he did very well at his lessons.

When Isaac was 14,
his stepfather died.
His mother moved back to Woolsthorpe.
Isaac left school to help her
on the farm
but he didn't like farming much.
He was too busy reading and thinking
to run a farm.
He was once fined for letting his sheep
break into a neighbour's field.

His uncle said
that Isaac should go to University.
In the end, his mother agreed.
After all, he wasn't much use
on the farm.

At the age of 18,
Isaac left his village
and went to Cambridge University.

3 Student Days

Isaac had very little money.
At first, he had to pay his way at University
by working as a servant.
He cleaned the rooms of the other students.
He made no friends.

Isaac did not like being poor.
He wanted to have some money
and he wanted to be respected.
The only way was to work hard.

He studied all the time.
He got interested in maths.
He also got interested in
the stars and planets.
Once, he nearly blinded himself
by staring at the sun.
He had to lie in a dark room
for three days
before his sight returned.

Isaac had a great talent for maths.
He soon understood
the most advanced maths of the time.

Then the Plague came to Cambridge.
The Plague was a deadly disease.
It killed thousands all over the country.
Cambridge University shut down.
The students were sent home.

Isaac went back to Woolsthorpe.
It was there, sitting under an apple tree,
that he made his great discovery of gravity.

Most people would have rushed
to tell the world of their discovery,
but not Isaac.
Perhaps he was shy.
He didn't tell anyone about his discovery.
He didn't publish his ideas
for another 22 years.

4 The Professor

When the University opened again,
Isaac went back.
But not as a student this time.
He was now so good at maths
that he was made Professor of Mathematics.
He was only 26 years old.

He no longer had to work as a servant.
As a Professor, he was paid by the University.
He gave lectures on maths to the students.
But his ideas were so advanced
that the students couldn't understand them.
They stopped coming to his lectures.
But Isaac didn't stop giving the lectures.
It was part of his job.
He gave them once a year, for 17 years,
to an empty hall.

Isaac was still working on his ideas.
He was interested in light.
He discovered that white light
is a mix of different colours.
If you pass sunlight through a prism
(a glass shape)
the light splits into
red, orange, yellow, green,
blue, indigo and violet.
These are the colours of the rainbow.
Isaac proved that white light
(the normal sunlight that we see)
is really a mix of these colours.
But still, he did not publish his ideas.

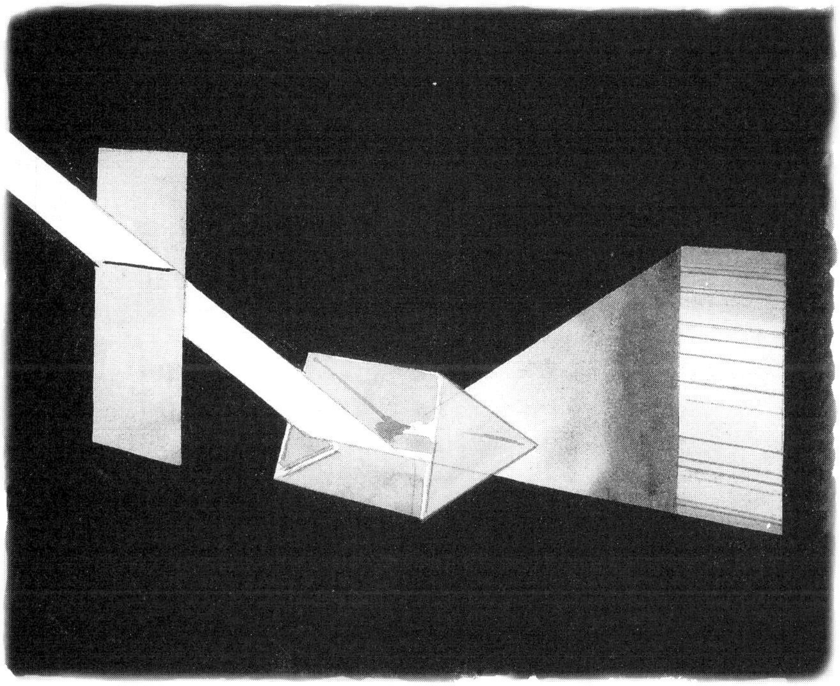

However, while he was working on light,
he invented a new telescope.
It was called a reflecting telescope.
He sent one to
the Royal Society
as a gift.

The Royal Society was
a group of top scientists.
They met to discuss new ideas.
They were impressed by Isaac's telescope.
It used a mirror to focus light
and it made things look 40 times bigger.
They asked Isaac to join the Royal Society.

The poor farmer's son
was now a Professor of Mathematics
and a Fellow of the Royal Society.

He had made it.

4 Isaac's Book

Isaac was now the greatest scientist
in the world.
The strange thing was,
hardly anyone knew it.
Hardly anyone had heard of him.
He had published nothing.

Only his colleagues in the Royal Society
guessed how advanced his ideas were.
They were always asking him to
publish his findings.
Isaac didn't want to.
He was shy.
He was afraid people would laugh at him.

He was still a very lonely man.
He had few friends.
Throughout his life,
he never had a girlfriend.
He found it very hard to trust people.

The nearest he had to a friend
at the Royal Society was Edmund Halley.
Halley was an astronomer.
He and Isaac were not close friends,
but Halley respected Isaac.
He knew how important Isaac's ideas were.
At last, he got Isaac to agree –
he would publish his ideas in a book.
Halley even paid
for the book to be published.

The book was called *Principia*.
It came out in 1687.
Isaac was 45 years old.

It contained all Isaac's ideas –
about gravity and about light.
It contained Isaac's famous Three Laws.

The First Law said:
If a thing is still, it will stay still,
unless a force moves it.
If it is moving, it will keep moving,
unless a force stops it.

The Second Law said:
If a thing is moving,
it will move faster
when a force pulls or pushes it.

The Third Law said:
Every action has an equal
and opposite reaction.
If you push something,
it pushes back.
This is why when you
push back against the side
of a swimming pool,
you move forward
through the water

Each law was proved with mathematics.
The book was a great success.
With *Principia,*
modern science had begun.

Isaac was now famous.
Scientists all over the world
read his work.
But none of them knew that Isaac
was interested in magic
as well as science.

6 A Secret

After *Principia,*
Isaac stopped studying science
for a while.
But he carried on doing alchemy.

Alchemy was the study
of how to turn lead into gold.
Alchemists also wanted to find
the secret of eternal life.
They heated up metals
and said spells over them
at full moon.
It wasn't science.
It was magic,
and, of course, it didn't work.

Isaac was sure he could make it work.
He had to keep it a secret.
If people had known
that the greatest scientist of the age
believed in magic,
they would have laughed at him.

Isaac had started alchemy
as a student.
He carried on all through his life.
but he never did manage
to turn lead into gold.

7 Public Life

In 1689, Isaac was elected MP
for Cambridge.
This was a new career for him.
He was not a great success as an MP.
He only ever spoke once in Parliament –
and that was when he asked someone
to close a window.

A year later, Isaac had a mental breakdown.
He became very depressed
and wrote strange letters to people he knew.
He accused one friend of
trying to get him involved with women.
This was not true, of course.
Isaac never got involved with women.
Perhaps he had the breakdown
because he was lonely.

However, he recovered quickly.
In 1699, he was given
an important public job.
He was made Warden of the Royal Mint.

This job put him in charge
of making all the coins
for the country.

He left Cambridge
and moved to London.

Isaac was very good at his job.
He was a very strict boss.
He made the Mint run much more smoothly.
He cracked down on forgers.
Many of them were caught and hanged.

In 1703, Isaac was made
President of the Royal Society.
The following year,
he published another book, *Opticks*.
This was all about his experiments with light.

Again, the book was a great success.
Isaac Newton was now at the height
of his fame.

8 Last Days

Being rich and famous
did not make Isaac easier to get on with.
He had never been good at making friends.
As he got older,
he became good at making enemies.

He ruled the Royal Society
with a rod of iron.
Nobody was allowed
to disagree with him.

He had long, bitter rows
with other scientists.

Some years earlier,
Isaac had discovered calculus –
an important new way of doing mathematics.
Another mathematician,
a German called Leibniz,
discovered it at the same time.
Isaac was very angry
and said Leibniz had stolen his idea.

He spent many years
writing angry letters to Leibniz about it,
until Leibniz died in 1716.

Isaac was getting old himself now.
His health began to fail.
He needed country air.
He moved to Kensington,
which was then a small village outside London.

Two years later, at the age of 85,
he died.

He was buried in Westminster Abbey.
All over Europe,
people paid tribute to him.

He had been the greatest scientist of his age.

But had he ever been happy?

ISAACVS NEWTON
HVMANI GENERIS DECVS

Key Dates

1642	Isaac Newton born on Christmas Day.
1645	Left with his grandmother when his mother married again.
1655	Went to King's School, Grantham. After three years, left to work on his mother's farm.
1661	Went to Trinity College, Cambridge.
1665	Discovered gravity, but did not publish his ideas.
1669	Became Professor of Mathematics at Cambridge.
1671	Invented reflecting telescope.
1672	Became Fellow of the Royal Society.
1687	Published his great work, *Principia*. Became internationally famous.
1695	Became Warden of the Royal Mint
1703	Elected President of the Royal Society
1704	Published *Opticks*.
1727	Died on 20 March. Buried in Westminster Abbey.